Life Around the World

What's Work Like Around the World?

By Kathleen Connors

New York

Published in 2022 by Cavendish Square Publishing, LLC
243 5th Avenue, Suite 136, New York, NY 10016

First Edition

Website: cavendishsq.com

Library of Congress Cataloging-in-Publication Data
Names: Connors, Kathleen, author.
Title: What's work like around the world? / Kathleen Connors.
Description: New York : Cavendish Square Publishing, [2022] | Series: Life around the world | Includes index.
Identifiers: LCCN 2020031840 | ISBN 9781502659521 (library binding) | ISBN 9781502659507 (paperback) | ISBN 9781502659514 (set) | ISBN 9781502659538 (ebook)
Subjects: LCSH: Work–Juvenile literature. | Occupations–Juvenile literature.
Classification: LCC HD4902.5 .C66 2022 | DDC 331.702–dc23
LC record available at https://lccn.loc.gov/2020031840

Editor: Kristen Nelson
Designer: Tanya Dellaccio

The photographs in this book are used by permission and through the courtesy of: Cover Syda Productions/Shutterstock.com; p. 5 (top) Zubin Shroff/Stone/Getty Images Plus/Getty Images; p. 5 (bottom) Miora Rajaonary/Moment/Getty Images; p. 7 Igor Alecsander/E+/Getty Images; p. 9 VCG/Visual China Group/Getty Images; p. 11 Majority World/Universal Images Group/Getty Images; p. 13 (top) Mint Images/Getty Images; p. 13 (bottom) Prasit photo/Moment/Getty Images; p. 15 alvarez/E+/Getty Images; p. 17 Luis Alvarez/DigitalVision/Getty Images; p. 19 Bloomberg/Getty Images; p. 21 fizkes/Shutterstock.com; p. 23 Beerpixs/Moment/Getty Images.

CPSIA compliance information: Batch #CS22CSQ: For further information contact Cavendish Square Publishing LLC, New York, New York, at 1-877-980-4450.

Printed in the United States of America

CONTENTS

Kinds of Work 4

Workdays and Workweeks 16

Around the World Work 22

Words to Know 24

Index 24

Kinds of Work

Life in countries around the world can be very different from place to place. However, people all over the world go to work to make money. Work means the jobs people do.

Some kinds of work happen all over the world. Farmers grow food for people to eat. What they grow depends on the weather and land where they are. Soybeans and sugarcane grow well in Brazil.

Farmers around the world raise animals too. In many countries, cows are raised for their milk. India **produces** the most milk. China raises the most chickens and produces the most eggs.

Teachers around the world help people learn new things. Their work can be very different, though. Teachers in the United States often use **technology** in class. In Afghanistan, some teachers don't even have books for their classes.

Chefs are people whose job it is to prepare food. However, a chef in France makes different food than one in Japan! A **sushi** chef, or *itame*, in Japan works for many years to become the best at making sushi.

Many people around the world today work with technology. They build and fix computers and computer **programs**. Their work can sometimes be done from anywhere. People may work together but be thousands of miles apart!

Workdays and Workweeks

Work around the world may be somewhat the same, but when it's done may be different. In Israel, the workweek is Sunday to Thursday. Workers are then off for Shabbat, or the holy day from Friday night to Saturday night.

How long a workday or workweek is also depends on where you live. Workers in South Korea have been known to work some of the longest hours. Mexico and Costa Rica had the next longest working hours.

In Sweden, coffee breaks are very important. Called *fika*, they happen twice a day for all workers. In countries where many Muslims live, workers stop at certain times throughout the day. They do this to **pray**.

Around the World Work

Some work takes people around the world! Photographers, or people who take pictures, may visit many countries. Writers may go to faraway places to report about life there. What kind of work do you want to do?

WORDS TO KNOW

pray: To speak to God.

produces: To be the place where something comes from.

programs: Sets of code that run on a computer and carry out certain tasks. Also called software.

sushi: A Japanese dish of cold cooked rice shaped in small cakes and topped or wrapped with other foods, such as pieces of raw fish.

technology: The way people do something and the tools they use.

INDEX

C

chefs, 12

F

farmers, 6, 8

P

photographers, 22

T

teachers, 10

technology, 10, 14

W

writers, 22